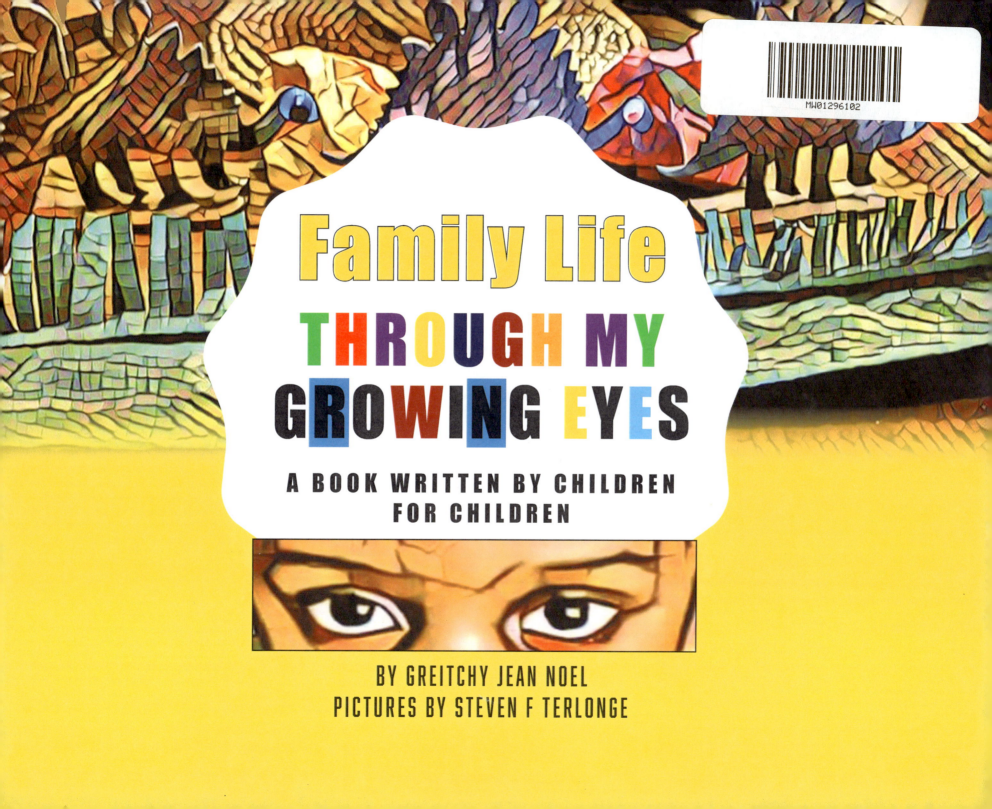

Family Life
THROUGH MY GROWING EYES

A BOOK WRITTEN BY CHILDREN FOR CHILDREN

BY GREITCHY JEAN NOEL
PICTURES BY STEVEN F TERLONGE

Xulon Press
2301 Lucien Way #415
Maitland, FL 32751
407.339.4217
www.xulonpress.com

© 2022 by Greitchy Jean Noel

All rights reserved solely by the author. The author guarantees all contents are original and do not infringe upon the legal rights of any other person or work. No part of this book may be reproduced in any form without the permission of the author.

Due to the changing nature of the Internet, if there are any web addresses, links, or URLs included in this manuscript, these may have been altered and may no longer be accessible. The views and opinions shared in this book belong solely to the author and do not necessarily reflect those of the publisher. The publisher therefore disclaims responsibility for the views or opinions expressed within the work.

Paperback ISBN-13: 978-1-6628-4183-5
eBook ISBN-13: 978-1-6628-4184-2

IN REMEMBRANCE OF GRANDMA

Heaven is a delightful dwelling because they have our Grandma.

ROLES OF THE FAMILY IN A CHILD'S GROWTH

When BORN, we join a group of one or more parents and their kids living together as one. As days, months, and years goes by, we are taught a tremendous amount of LESSONS from our mom and dad. Our family's teachings sets the BASIS that shapes up our morals, our GROWTH, and our sanctuary.

THE TAG

- People often think the first child in any family are **mature.** They're often leading the pack, easy to rely on, and are almost always making efforts to making mommy and daddy proud.

THE OLDEST...

WHAT IS IT LIKE?

WHAT ARE SOME GOOD AND BAD THINGS YOU GO THROUGH AS THE FIRST BORN?

ZION-
"HIGHEST POINT"

I am the 1st born child. I am 8 years old, the one **opened the womb** of my mother as she to call it. I have one little brother and one sister. As a big brother, I **tutor** my siblings everything I know and I try to be an example a good big brother. Apart from our mother father, my brother and sister look to me for answers. Being a big brother is both awesome and trying. I find that at times it can be **alot** because they copy everything that I do, it leaves me with little free time to watch my favorite cartoon shows; Sid the Science Kid, Wild Kratts, and play my favorite sport of basketball by myself.

WHAT I'VE LEARNED SO FAR...

My starring role in my family is to be there for my little brother and sister-rain or shine, and love them through life the best way I can. They are my favorite and I wouldn't trade them for **anything** in this world!

THE RECEIVED IDEA

MIDDLE KIDS OFTEN FEEL **IGNORED** AND OFTEN GROW ANGRY OF ALL MOM AND DAD'S CARE GIVEN TO THE OLDEST AND THE BABY OF THE FAMILY, AND FEEL **SHORT-CHANGED.**

WHAT IS IT LIKE BEING THE MIDDLE CHILD?

THE GOOD, THE BAD, AND THE UGLY

ETHAN – "STRONG, OPTIMISTIC, & SOLID"

I am the **2nd** born child. I am 6 years old, the one who have little **rights** of my oldest brother (Zion) or the **treat** of being the youngest sister (Kai). I am the middle child, I have a big brother and a little sister. As the middle child, I share some of the same duties as Zion when it comes to my baby sister. I play with her and teach her what I know and I correct her when she's off beam. I have the benefit of being close to both my big brother and my baby sister. I'm the one that brings **balance** and I am able to see both views of an older brother and a little one too. Being in the middle is both cool and hard. I have to say that sometimes I feel **overshadowed** by one or both of my siblings and when I do- my mommy and daddy encourages me to talk about it as a family. At this time, my favorite cartoon shows are Amazing Spiderman and Teenage Mutant Ninja Turtles and my favorite sport is soccer and with my favorite things, I sometimes have to share my time and mediate between my older brother and younger sister.

THE UPS & DOWNS...

WHAT I'VE LEARNED SO FAR...

- My **part** in my family is to have **more freedom** and **less pressure** with more things. It's not so bad after all,

- I 2nd that!

THE IDEAS

YOUNGER CHILDREN IN THE FAMILY ARE ALSO OFTEN DESCRIBED AS **DETERMINED**, WILLING TO TAKE UNNECESSARY RISKS IN ORDER TO GET WHAT THEY WANT BY WEARING THEIR PARENTS DOWN.

THE HIGHS AND LOWS AS BABY OF THE FAMILY?

DO TELL!

KAI - "WARRIOR"

I am the **last** of the family pack. I am 4 years old, the one that **could hardly contain her glee over** being last. I have 2 big brothers that I love both spending time with and showing that I am big enough to do big kid things! As the baby, my brothers have me ask our parents for things that would typically get a NO. Sometimes being younger are both **great** and **unfair.** My brothers sometimes both pick on me and treat me like a little o'le baby! My favorite cartoon shows are PJ Masks and Peppa Pig and because of this, my brothers and I fight over the remote every time causing mommy to say if we don't take turns watching our shows, it will result with her taking the remote!

MY TAKE...

LESSONS LEARNED SO FAR...

- My role in our family is just as needed as the first and second born. I am the baby of the family, **it is an HONOR!**

AFFIRMATIONS FOR A BALANCE IN THE FAMILY DYNAMIC

- Family roles have **good** and **bad** pieces to them. The key is figuring out how good and or bad these roles work in your dynamic. **Helpful affirmations** increases your self-esteem, your ability to accomplish goals, and life around you.

WHAT AFFIRMATIONS DO YOU HAVE?

PLEASE SHARE!

ZION'S DAY TO DAY AFFIRMATIONS AS THE OLDEST CHILD

- I am a **front-runner!**
- I am a **good influence** on others!
- I don't need to be perfect, **I just need to be perfectly ME!**
- I am both **special** and **unique!**

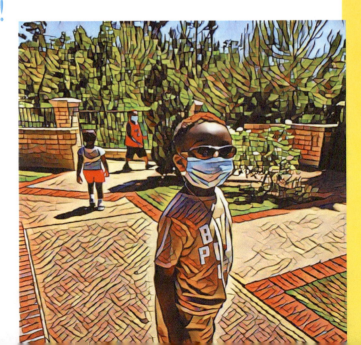

ETHAN'S DAY TO DAY AFFIRMATIONS AS MIDDLE CHILD

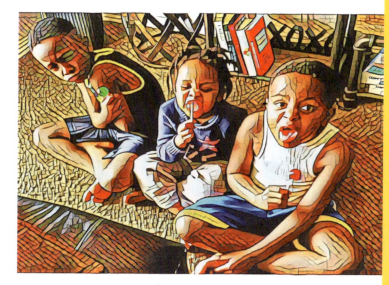

- I **MATTER!**
- I choose my own **ATTITUDE!**
- I am **RESOURCEFUL!**
- I am **LOVED!**
- I am stretched both ways but **WILL NOT BREAK!**

KAI'S DAY TO DAY AFFIRMATIONS AS THE BABY OF THE FAMILY

- I am **ME!**
- I have my **OWN** voice!
- Sometimes I will **WIN** & sometimes I will LOSE!
- I am **BOLD!**

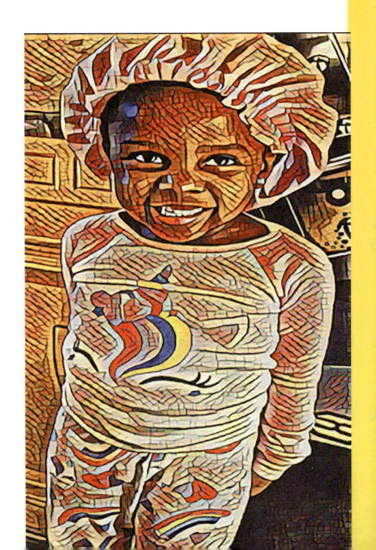

FAMILY ROLES PLAY A PART TO THE TOTAL FAMILY DYNAMIC

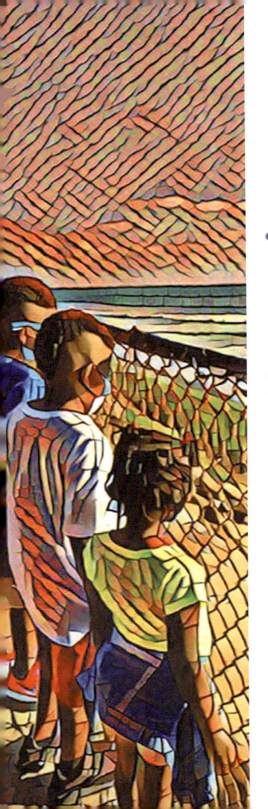

GOLDEN NUGGETS

- We all have different roles within our family. Our part in our family are needed for a strong family structure. Whether you are **1st** like ME - **Zion**, **2nd** like ME - **Ethan**, or **3rd** like ME - **Kai**, know that there will be both good and bad times. Most importantly, know that **you matter** to those around you and to the world!!!

CPSIA information can be obtained
at www.ICGtesting.com
Printed in the USA
LVRC090746030322
712534LV00003B/72

9 781662 841835